THE
LITTLE LOCAL
MAINE
COOKBOOK

THE
LITTLE LOCAL
MAINE
COOKBOOK

Recipes for Classic Dishes

ANNIE B. COPPS

THE COUNTRYMAN PRESS
A division of W. W. Norton & Company
Independent Publishers Since 1923

Copyright © 2019 by Connected Dots Media
Illustrations by Courtney Jentzen

For information about permission to reproduce selections
from this book, write to Permissions, The Countryman Press,
500 Fifth Avenue, New York, NY 10110

For information about special discounts for bulk purchases,
please contact W. W. Norton Special Sales at
specialsales@wwnorton.com or 800-233-4830

Manufacturing by Versa Press
Book design by Debbie Berne
Production manager: Devon Zahn

Library of Congress Cataloging-in-Publication Data

Names: Copps, Annie B., author. | Jentzen, Courtney, illustrator.
Title: The little local Maine cookbook / Annie B. Copps ; illustrations by
    Courtney Jentzen.
Description: New York, NY : Countryman Press, [2019] | Includes
    bibliographical references and index.
Identifiers: LCCN 2019006205 | ISBN 9781682684177 (hardcover : alk. paper)
Subjects: LCSH: Cooking—Maine. | Cooking, American—New England
    style. | LCGFT: Cookbooks.
Classification: LCC TX715 .C7924 2018 | DDC 641.59741—dc23
LC record available at https://lccn.loc.gov/2019006205

The Countryman Press
www.countrymanpress.com

A division of W. W. Norton & Company, Inc.
500 Fifth Avenue, New York, NY 10110
www.wwnorton.com

978-1-68268-417-7

10 9 8 7 6 5 4 3 2

For Rick Johnson, who loved Maine

CONTENTS

Desserts

INTRODUCTION

The state of Maine is an extraordinary part of the world packed with miles of breathtaking and diverse natural beauty, as well as a strong and proud culture that is equally diverse and beautiful. From the town of Eastport, where the sunrise is always the first in the nation, to the 250 miles of rocky coastline to the interior full of snow-covered mountains and deep woods, it's easy to understand why Maine is nicknamed "Vacationland" and how Winslow Homer, Andrew Wyeth, and Stephen King found so much inspiration there.

The gracious rewards of the sea and the fertile land have long provided delicious, fresh seafood and produce for the people of Maine and those who come to visit it. Neptune has been kind to the hardworking men and women who make their living from the clean, cold waters of Maine, and those working the fields benefit from its rich, fertile soil. When most people think of lobsters, or of blueberries or potatoes, Maine comes to mind. But Maine cuisine offers so much more. Traditional recipes dating back to the time of the earliest settlers are still served in many homes, and some Maine kitchens are cooking up head-turning meals using locally sourced ingredients with contemporary twists.

This little book celebrates the bounty of Maine and the talented people who make their living harvesting from its land and sea, as well as the many home cooks and professional chefs who keep Maine cuisine relevant.

APPETIZERS
AND
DRINKS

OYSTERS THREE WAYS
Raw, Roasted, and Fried

Of all the ingredients found around the globe, an oyster is best at telling you exactly where it's from. On the East Coast, most of the oysters are from the same species *Crassostrea virginica*, but their breeding ground, shape, and size all play roles in how they taste. An oyster's flavor differs depending on the temperature and salinity of the water in which it breeds, what else grows in those same waters, and the local tides and currents. The cold and briny Atlantic Ocean and the rivers of Maine produce world-class oysters, and depending on where and when they are harvested, they vary in taste, texture, and size.

The cold waters of the Damariscotta River produce wonderful oysters from many spots along its banks, such as Pemaquid, Wawenauk, or Glidden Point. The Bagaduce River, Taunton Bay, and hundreds of other locations around Maine are great sources for oysters as well.

Purists prefer oysters served raw, on the half shell, and with a squeeze of lemon juice or a simple mignonette sauce, but their lightly salty flavor and silky texture are also excellent fried or roasted.

RAW ON THE HALF SHELL
WITH MIGNONETTE SAUCE

Makes 12 pieces

¼ cup apple cider vinegar, red wine vinegar, or Champagne vinegar

1 tablespoon finely minced shallots

¼ teaspoon coarsely ground fresh black pepper

12 medium (3-inch) fresh Maine oysters, shucked and on the half shell

1 To make the mignonette sauce, in the small bowl, stir together the vinegar, shallots, and black pepper. Set aside.

2 Arrange the oysters in their half shells in a shallow bowl or platter on a bed of ice. Spoon some mignonette sauce on top of each oyster. Serve chilled.

• • •

BACON WRAPPED AND ROASTED

Makes 12 pieces

12 medium (3-inch) fresh Maine oysters, shucked, oyster meat reserved (clean and reserve one shell from each oyster)

¾ cup cream cheese or mascarpone cheese

3 tablespoons chopped fresh flat-leaf parsley

2 tablespoons minced scallions (about 2), white and light green parts only

Freshly squeezed juice of 1 lemon

12 thinly sliced strips bacon, pancetta, or prosciutto (4 inches long by 2 inches wide)

1 Heat the oven to 450°F.

2 Place reserved oyster shells on a salt-lined baking sheet to keep them stable.

Continued

3 In a small bowl, combine the cream cheese, 2 tablespoons parsley, the scallions, and 2 teaspoons lemon juice. Set aside.

4 Lay the bacon strips vertically on a clean surface. Gently shake loose any moisture from a piece of oyster meat and place on the bottom end of a strip of bacon. Spoon a small dollop of the cheese mixture on the oyster meat. Carefully roll the bacon over the oyster and cheese and place the rolled package back in a reserved shell, bacon seam side down. Repeat with the remaining oysters.

5 Place in the oven and roast 10 to 15 minutes, until the bacon is crisped and lightly browned.

6 Remove from the oven and transfer to a salt-lined plate or platter. Scatter the remaining lemon juice and sprinkle the remaining parsley over the oysters. Serve immediately.

· · ·

FRIED WITH TARTAR SAUCE

Makes 12 pieces

12 medium (3-inch) fresh Maine oysters, shucked, clean, and reserve one shell from each	Kosher or sea salt
	Freshly ground black pepper
2 cups buttermilk	Vegetable oil for frying
1 cup cornmeal	Tartar Sauce for serving (recipe follows)
1 cup all-purpose flour	Garnish: fresh chopped parsley

1 In a medium bowl, soak oysters in buttermilk for about 20 minutes but not more than 1 hour.

2 In a second, larger bowl, combine the cornmeal, the flour, and a pinch each of salt and black pepper.

3 In a deep fryer or deep-sided cast-iron pan, heat 3 inches of oil to 375°F.

4 Gently shake excess buttermilk off the oysters and dredge the oysters in the flour mixture until completely coated. Gently shake off any excess flour and carefully slip the oysters into hot oil, being careful not to overcrowd the pan. Fry until golden brown, 3 to 4 minutes. Remove the oysters with a slotted spoon and drain on a paper towel–lined plate; season with salt while still hot.

5 Make a ¼-inch layer of salt on a plate or platter and nest the shells in the salt. Place 1 tablespoon Tartar Sauce in each shell, place a hot oyster on top, and sprinkle with parsley. Serve immediately.

• • •

TARTAR SAUCE

Makes about 1 cup

1 cup mayonnaise

2 tablespoons sweet pickle relish or finely chopped pickles

1 teaspoon fresh lemon juice

¼ teaspoon Tabasco sauce

In a bowl, stir together all the ingredients until well combined. Refrigerate until ready to use.

SHRIMP AND CORN FRITTERS

Makes about 3 dozen

Tiny ½-inch Maine shrimp are prized for their sweet flavor. They are also a challenge to catch. Shrimp season usually runs from December to April, when the ocean is unpredictable, icy cold, and windy—it's no easy feat to take a boat out for shrimping in that weather. If these very special gems are unavailable, substitute with your favorite shrimp or lobster.

1 cup all-purpose flour

½ teaspoon kosher or sea salt, plus more for seasoning

1 teaspoon baking powder

1 tablespoon chopped fresh parsley, plus more for garnish

1 tablespoon chopped fresh chives

Freshly grated zest of 1 lemon

¼ teaspoon freshly ground black pepper

Freshly squeezed juice of 1 lemon

Whole milk as needed

1 large egg, beaten

1 pound (about 2 cups) raw Maine shrimp (or other shrimp or lobster cut into ½-inch pieces), peeled

1 cup corn kernels, fresh or frozen and defrosted

Vegetable oil for frying

Herb Dipping Sauce (recipe follows) for serving

1 In a medium bowl, whisk together the flour, the baking powder, and the ½ teaspoon salt. Add the herbs, lemon zest, and black pepper.

2 In a measuring cup, combine the lemon juice and enough milk to equal ⅓ cup of liquid total. Whisk the egg into the milk mixture.

3 Add the wet ingredients to the dry ingredients and mix just until combined. Fold in the shrimp and corn kernels.

4 In a deep fryer or deep-sided cast-iron pan, heat 3 inches of oil to 375°F.

5 Carefully spoon about 1 tablespoon batter into the oil, being careful not to overcrowd the pan. Fry until golden brown, 3 to 4 minutes. Remove with a slotted spoon and drain on paper towel–lined plate; season with salt while still hot. Sprinkle with the remaining parsley.

6 When cool enough to handle, plate and serve with Herb Dipping Sauce.

• • •

HERB DIPPING SAUCE

Makes about 1 cup

½ cup mayonnaise

½ cup sour cream

1 clove garlic, minced

1 teaspoon each (or more to taste) chopped fresh dill, parsley, and chives

2 scallions, finely chopped

1 squeeze fresh lemon juice

Freshly grated zest of ½ lemon

Few drops Tabasco sauce

In a bowl, stir together all the ingredients until well combined. Refrigerate until ready to use.

ROASTED MUSSELS WITH GARLIC SCAPE BUTTER

Makes 6 servings

Although mussels from Maine have a shiny shell that appears black, they are often called blue mussels because the color is actually a very deep indigo. Mussels are versatile and delicious whether they're grilled, steamed, or quickly roasted; but like most shellfish, they don't take long to cook and get rubbery when overdone.

Garlic scapes are the long, thin stalks that grow from garlic plant bulbs into elegant curlicues. Snipping the scapes in early summer, like pruning a rose bush, encourages the garlic to focus its energy underground and generate larger, tastier garlic bulbs later in the season. Scapes also taste terrific—garlicky, but less intense. Serve with some bread to sop up the irresistible pan sauce.

½ pound (2 sticks) unsalted butter at room temperature, cut into 2-inch pieces

5 to 6 garlic scapes, trimmed and finely chopped

2 teaspoons freshly grated lemon zest

1 clove garlic, minced

½ teaspoon red pepper flakes

3½ pounds fresh Maine mussels, scrubbed and de-bearded

½ cup dry white wine

Garnish: ¼ cup minced parsley

1 loaf thick-crusted French or Italian bread for serving

1 Heat the oven to 400°F.

2 In a small bowl, mash together the butter, scapes, lemon zest, garlic, and red pepper flakes.

3 Evenly divide the seasoned butter in teaspoon-sized portions on the bottom of a large, rimmed baking dish. Scatter the mussels over the butter and pour over the wine.

4 Place in the oven until most mussels have opened, about 10 minutes.

5 Shake the pan to evenly distribute the sauce so it gets inside the shells, then return to the oven for 3 or 4 more minutes. Discard any unopened mussels, garnish with parsley, and serve hot with bread.

DOWN EAST LOBSTER TOMALLEY DIP

Makes about 2 cups

While most people love lobster, "true" lobster lovers go for the tomalley, the soft green inside bits that are the creature's liver and pancreas (aka the hepatopancreas). Tomalley has a particular and very intense lobster flavor, as well as a very creamy texture.

If you want to make this recipe without getting a whole lobster, most fishmongers sell tomalley separately.

2 tablespoons unsalted butter

½ cup (about 1 medium) rinsed and roughly chopped leek, white and light green parts only

½ cup roughly chopped fennel bulb (reserve a few fronds for garnish)

½ cup lobster tomalley

2 tablespoons Pernod

½ cup cream cheese

Garnish: 1 tablespoon chopped fresh parsley

Saltine crackers for serving

1 In a medium sauté pan over low heat, melt the butter. Add the leek and fennel, stir well to coat, and slowly cook, stirring occasionally, until vegetables are translucent, softened, and fragrant, about 30 minutes (be careful not to brown them).

2 Stir in the tomalley and cook, stirring occasionally, until opaque and "dull" in color, about 10 minutes (it's okay if it breaks apart).

3 Raise the heat to medium-high and add the Pernod. Cook, stirring occasionally, until the pan is almost dry. Remove from the heat and let cool to room temperature.

4 In the bowl of a food processor or using an immersion blender, puree the contents of the pan. Fold in the cream cheese and parsley. Serve with saltines.

Note: A dear friend's grandmother, a Bailey Island resident, used to eat the tomalley raw on Saltine crackers but it may be more palatable whisked into sauces or in this delicious Down East dip (served on a Saltine).

MY BLUE HEAVEN BLUEBERRY COCKTAIL

Makes 2 servings

Wild blueberries, along with cranberries and Concord grapes, are among the fruits native to North America. Also called lowbush blueberries, wild blueberries are the state fruit of Maine. Compared to their cultivated cousins, wild blueberries are smaller, sweeter, firmer, and have a vibrant purple hue, all because they are harvested by hand from wild bushes rather than from fields pumped full of water. And because they are hand-collected and more delicate, most Maine blueberries don't make it across the state line.

2 tablespoons Maine blueberries, plus more for garnish

1 tablespoon strained Blueberry Jam (page 70)

4 or 5 ice cubes, plus more for serving

2 ounces light rum

2 teaspoons fresh lemon juice

2 ounces club soda

Garnish: 2 lemon slices

1 In a cocktail shaker, using a muddler or wooden spoon, muddle together the 2 tablespoons blueberries, the blueberry jam, and the 4 or 5 ice cubes until the berries and ice are crushed. Stir in the rum and lemon juice, and then gently stir in the club soda.

2 Add 3 or 4 ice cubes to two Collins glasses and strain into the glasses. Garnish with 2 or 3 more blueberries and a lemon slice and serve.

MAINE MOXIE
MANHATTAN

Makes 2 servings

Moxie is Maine's official soft drink. It's been in production since 1886, making it one of the oldest mass-produced beverages in the United States. Moxie was recently purchased by Coca Cola, but its secret formula remains unchanged. A person with a lot of gumption or pluck is said to be full of "moxie," and the drink bears that out with its high caffeine and carbonation content.

Herbal, bitter, and effervescent, Moxie got its start as a medicinal elixir. Made from gentian root, it was advertised as an aid for digestion. Moxie goes in and out of fashion, but it can always be found on market shelves from Machias to Kennebunkport. Thanks to the cocktail cultural revival, it's enjoying a bit of a renaissance these days, as it makes a perfect mixer or is great as a bitter. A lot of Mainers mix Moxie with Allen's brand coffee brandy and some ice cubes as an afternoon pick-me-up. Here, the Maine classic is put to use in a twist on the classic Manhattan.

4 ounces bourbon or rye	2 ounces Moxie
2 ounces sweet vermouth	Garnish: fresh Maine blueberries

In a cocktail shaker half-filled with ice, stir together the bourbon, sweet vermouth, and Moxie. Strain into chilled martini glasses or ice-filled Collins glasses. Garnish with blueberries and serve.

SPICED APPLE CIDER

Makes 4 servings

Come fall, wild blueberries take a backseat to another New England favorite: apples. Hundreds of varieties grow in Maine, and determining the type to choose is a matter of flavor and how you plan to use them. McIntosh is an easy-to-find all-around favorite that's great for eating or for making cider or sauce, but the variety isn't great for pies because they lose their shape. Sweet and juicy Macouns are also good for baking or eating out of hand. "Antique" varietals, such as Roxbury Russets and Spitzenburgs, are special treats. Spencers store for a long time and work well in baking or for eating raw, while Cox's Orange Pippin is a prized variety for desserts.

As the weather cools, a hot or cold glass of apple cider is refreshing and delicious. Add a splash of rum for an adult version.

1 medium orange, well-scrubbed

10 medium apples, washed and quartered (skins on, seeds and cores discarded)

3 cinnamon sticks

3 or 4 whole cloves

About 2 tablespoons granulated sugar (more or less depending on the sweetness of the apples and your preference)

1 Grate and reserve the orange zest. Discard the peel and roughly chop the flesh; discard any seeds.

2 In a large, heavy-bottomed pot, combine all the ingredients, including the reserved orange zest. Add enough water to cover the fruit, cover, and place over medium-high heat. Bring to a boil and then reduce the heat to very low. Gently simmer, covered and stirring occasionally, 4 to 5 hours, or transfer to a slow cooker and cook on low for 5 or 6 hours.

3 Gently mash the fruit. Cover and cook on low for 1 more hour. Remove from the heat.

4 Carefully strain the chunky liquid though a fine-mesh sieve lined with cheesecloth into a large pot or pitcher. Serve the cider warm or set aside to cool completely and then chill.

SALADS, SOUPS, AND SIDES

PICKLED FIDDLEHEAD FERNS

Makes six ½-pint jars

Maine winters are long, so when the first fiddlehead ferns emerge from the cold, hard soil, it's cause for celebration. Foragers search for them where they grow wild, along river banks and in damp forests, but exactly where tends to be a well-kept secret. They are easily cultivated for home gardens.

Fiddleheads get their name from their tightly curled tops (the unopened fronds of the ostrich fern), which resemble the elegant carved wooden neck of a violin. Their flavor is unique but similar to that of an artichoke. Fiddleheads are great sautéed in butter with a bit of lemon, but pickling them gives them a longer shelf life. Try them on a cheese plate or even as a fun garnish for a martini.

1 pound fiddlehead ferns, washed and trimmed of any brown bits

3 cups apple cider vinegar or white wine vinegar

2 cups water

½ cup honey

¼ cup kosher or sea salt

2 dozen scallions, root ends trimmed, sliced in half widthwise

6 cloves garlic, peeled and lightly crushed

1 tablespoon whole black peppercorns, lightly crushed

2 teaspoons whole mustard seeds, lightly crushed

2 teaspoons whole coriander seeds, lightly crushed

2 teaspoons whole cumin seeds, lightly crushed

1 teaspoon whole red pepper flakes, lightly crushed

1 Bring a large pot of water to a boil. Add the cleaned and trimmed fiddleheads and cook for 2 minutes. Using a slotted spoon, remove the fiddleheads and plunge them in a bowl of ice water for 1 minute. Remove and reserve.

2 In a medium saucepan over high heat, combine the vinegar, water, honey, and salt and bring to a boil. Reduce the heat to a very gentle simmer until ready to use.

3 Line up six sterilized ½-pint glass canning jars and lids. Evenly divide the scallions; garlic; peppercorns; mustard, coriander, and cumin seeds; and red pepper flakes among the jars. Evenly divide the reserved fiddleheads among the jars.

4 Pour the hot pickling liquid over the vegetables, covering them completely and leaving ½ inch of head space in each jar. Gently tap each jar on a counter to force out air bubbles and wipe rims with a clean towel. Apply the lid and ring to each jar and process jars in boiling water for 10 minutes. Remove the jars and let cool.

5 Properly sealed, jars can be stored 6 to 8 months; unsealed or unprocessed jars must be refrigerated. Let the fiddleheads pickle for at least 1 week before eating.

POTATOES AU GRATIN

Makes 12 servings

It didn't take long for the Irish immigrants who came to Aroostook County in the eighteenth century to figure out that the forests they settled near had rich—albeit rocky—soil. Long summer days and cool nights created optimal potato-growing conditions, and soon Maine was producing more potatoes than any other state in the nation.

Today, Maine grows hundreds of types of potatoes, each with a different flavor and texture. Just about any potato will taste good in this recipe—anything from all-purpose Kennebecs and Carolas to starchy Green Mountains, Irish Cobblers, or Bintjes. The best choices are spring potatoes that had not been harvested the previous fall and spent the winter underground.

2 cups heavy cream	6 tablespoons unsalted butter
4 or 5 sprigs fresh thyme	2½ pounds potatoes, sliced ⅛ inch thick (peeled or unpeeled)
2 cloves garlic, peeled and lightly crushed	Kosher or sea salt
1 bay leaf, torn in half	White pepper
Few grates whole nutmeg	

1 Heat the oven to 350°F.

2 In a medium saucepan over medium-low heat, combine the cream, the thyme, 1 clove garlic, the bay leaf, and the nutmeg. Bring to a gentle simmer and cook until garlic is fragrant, about 10 minutes. Remove from the heat and set aside.

3 Rub the remaining clove of garlic around the inside of an 8-inch square, 2-inch deep baking pan. Rub 1 tablespoon butter inside the dish.

4 Strain the cream, discarding the solids, and pour a thin layer of it on the bottom of the baking pan. Shingle a single layer of sliced potatoes on top. Dot with some butter, lightly season with the salt and white pepper, and pour on another thin layer of cream. Repeat until all the potatoes are used, reserving about 2 teaspoons butter. Pour any remaining cream on top.

5 Grease a sheet of foil with the remaining butter and place it over the pan, butter side down. Seal it tightly and bake 45 minutes. Carefully remove the foil, raise the temperature to 400°F, and return to the oven until lightly browned on top, about 15 minutes. Remove from the oven and let rest 10 minutes before serving.

FISH CHOWDER

Makes 8 servings

The creation of European fishermen, chowder comes from the French *chaudiere*, a quick on-the-boat stew of hearty ingredients including whatever fresh fish or shellfish was captured that morning. In coastal Maine, it was an inexpensive way to feed a big family a nutritious meal. Traditionally, fish chowder is made with haddock and milk, but the variations are endless. This recipe is brothy, light, and simple, but also deeply flavorful and filling.

6 ounces unflavored slab bacon, diced into ¼-inch cubes	Freshly ground black pepper
2 cups finely diced onions (about 2 medium)	4 cups fish broth
1 tablespoon unsalted butter	4 to 5 sprigs fresh thyme
2 cups finely chopped yellow onions (about 2 medium)	2 bay leaves, broken in half
1 pound Maine russet potatoes, peeled and diced into ¼-inch cubes	1½ cups heavy cream
	1 cup whole milk
Kosher or sea salt	2 pounds fresh haddock, cut into 1-inch pieces
	Garnish: chopped fresh parsley

1 Place the bacon in a large, heavy-bottomed stockpot over medium heat and cook, stirring often, until lightly browned and the fat is rendered. Remove with a slotted spoon and drain on a paper towel-lined plate.

2 Reduce the heat to medium-low, add the onions and butter, and cook gently until the onions are softened and translucent, about 10 minutes, taking care not to brown them.

3 Add the diced potatoes and season with salt and black pepper; stir to coat and cook until the flavors absorb, 3 or 4 minutes, taking care not to brown them.

4 Add the fish broth, thyme, and bay leaves and raise the heat to a gentle simmer. Cover and let cook until the potatoes are fork tender, about 8 minutes.

5 In a separate pan over low heat, combine the cream and milk and cook until warm. Add the warm cream mixture and fish to the stockpot and gently stir to combine. Gently simmer about 10 minutes, until fish is cooked through (firm and opaque). Remove from the heat and remove and discard the thyme and bay leaves and gently stir in the reserved bacon. Taste and adjust seasoning with salt and black pepper.

6 Ladle into serving bowls and garnish with parsley. Serve.

LOBSTER BISQUE

Makes 6 servings

Enjoying lobster can be as simple as mixing a few ingredients together for a Lobster Roll (page 48), but if you're willing to invest some time, an elegant, silky-smooth bisque will extract the deepest, richest essence of the lobster.

If you are uncomfortable cutting up a live lobster, have your fishmonger do it for you, but be sure you are ready to use the lobster pieces right away.

¼ cup vegetable oil	3 sprigs fresh thyme
2 1½-pound live lobsters (body and tail, claws separated)	2 tablespoons tomato paste
	½ cup brandy or Cognac
1 cup finely chopped yellow onion or leek (white and light green parts only)	2 quarts heavy cream
	1½ teaspoons sherry vinegar

1 Heat the oil in a large, heavy-bottomed saucepan over medium heat. Add the lobster pieces, onion, and thyme and sauté until the lobster shells turn red and the meat is opaque, about 8 minutes.

2 Add the tomato paste and cook, stirring often, until slightly browned, about 3 minutes. Remove from the heat and add the brandy. Using a long match, carefully ignite the brandy and cook off the alcohol. After the flames have subsided, return to medium heat and cook, stirring constantly, until the liquid has reduced to about 1 tablespoon, 3 to 5 minutes. Stir in the cream and bring to a gentle simmer. Cook until the bisque thickens and the flavors have fully developed; 30 to 40 minutes. Remove from the heat.

3 Using tongs, transfer the lobster pieces to a plate and let cool slightly. When cool enough to handle, remove the meat from tail, claws, and knuckle shells; discard the shells and bodies. Chop the larger pieces of meat into 1-inch pieces and return the meat to the pan. Stir in the sherry vinegar and ladle into bowls. Serve.

MAINE CRAB SALAD–STUFFED AVOCADO

Makes 4 servings

Maine crabmeat comes from two different species—Jonah and rock crab—and most will agree the best crabs come from Penobscot Bay. Jonah crabs are a bit larger; are reddish in color; have large, black-tipped claws; and are found out to sea a bit. Smaller rock crabs live closer to shore, in bays and rivers. A few years ago, Rod Mitchell of Browne Trading Seafoods took a risk and began marketing rock crab as "peekytoe" crab, and it skyrocketed in popularity.

Avocados filled with crab salad may be a bit retro, but the two get along so well. You can also serve this salad on its own, with crusty bread.

2 tablespoons sherry vinegar, plus more for drizzling

1 tablespoon Dijon mustard

2 tablespoons extra virgin olive oil

8 ounces fresh, wild-caught crab meat, fully cooked

¼ cup finely diced cucumber

¼ cup finely diced red bell pepper

¼ cup cooked corn

1 tablespoon finely chopped scallions, plus more for garnish

2 ripe avocados

Kosher or sea salt

Freshly ground black pepper

1 In a medium mixing bowl, whisk together the 2 tablespoons sherry vinegar and the mustard. Slowly drizzle in the olive oil while whisking constantly.

2 In a separate small bowl, place the crab meat and, using your fingers, carefully remove and discard any pieces of shell or cartilage. Break the meat into small pieces. Add the crab to the mixing bowl, along with the cucumber, pepper, corn, and the 1 tablespoon scallions. Gently stir to combine.

3 Cut each avocado in half lengthwise, remove the pit, and scoop the flesh into a small bowl, reserving the skins. Mash the avocado and season with salt and black pepper.

4 Divide the mashed avocado among the reserved avocado skins and carefully top each with the crab salad. Drizzle a touch of sherry vinegar over the top and garnish with scallions. Serve.

BROWN BREAD

Makes 2 loaves

This distinct, dark, and rich bread was a favorite of the colonists. Brown bread loaves are traditionally steamed in 1-pound coffee cans, but this recipe is adjusted to bake in two 28-ounce cans, which are easier to find. This recipe includes wheat flour, for better loaf structure, but the traditional recipe relied on cornmeal, as it took awhile to get wheat growing in New England. This bread is traditionally served with Baked Beans (page 40).

About 1 tablespoon vegetable oil for greasing

1 cup rye flour

½ cup whole wheat flour

¾ cup (3¾ ounces) fine cornmeal

1 teaspoon baking soda

1 teaspoon kosher or sea salt

1½ cups buttermilk

⅔ cup molasses

3 tablespoons unsalted butter room temperature, melted and cooled to room temperature

¾ cup raisins or sultanas

Cream cheese or cooked Baked Beans (page 40) for serving

1 In a large stockpot over high heat, bring about 2 quarts of water to a simmer.

2 With the oil, lightly grease two 28-ounce, pristinely clean cans with their labels removed. Using one of the cans as a guide, trace and cut out 2 rounds of parchment paper. Lightly grease one side of each piece of parchment and place them, greased-side up, in the bottoms of the cans. Cut 2 squares of aluminum foil large enough to fit over the can tops. Lightly grease the foil and set aside. Cut two lengths of kitchen twine twice as long as the diameter of the cans; set aside.

3 In a large bowl, whisk together the rye and whole wheat flours, cornmeal, baking soda, and salt. In a separate medium bowl, combine the buttermilk, molasses, butter, and raisins. Add the buttermilk mixture to the flour mixture and stir just until combined and uniformly moist.

4 Evenly divide the batter between the prepared cans. Lay the aluminum foil squares, oil side down, on the cans' tops and attach using twine.

5 Carefully lower the cans into the simmering water (the water will need to come about halfway up the can sides). Cover and gently simmer 2 hours; periodically check the water level and add more as necessary.

6 Carefully remove the cans from the water bath and place on a cooling rack for 30 minutes. Remove the breads from the cans and let cool completely. Serve with cream cheese or baked beans.

BAKED BEANS

Makes 6 to 8 servings

For many Maine families, the traditional dinner schedule was: a boiled dinner midweek, followed by leftovers; fish chowder on Friday (in observance of the Catholic prohibition of meat on that day); baked beans on Saturday; and leftover baked beans on Sunday, so Mom could get a break and go to church. Mainers take their beans seriously, from how they are cooked to the type of beans used. The most popular Maine-grown beans are Marfax and Yellow Eyes, followed by Soldier, Jacob's Cattle, Cranberry, and Swedish Brown. (Don't tell this to a Mainer, but cannellini and other small beans work well, too.) Older baked bean recipes are quite sweet, but this version dials back the maple syrup and brown sugar; add more sugar if you prefer it.

The beans and all their flavorings were traditionally placed in a clay pot and slow-cooked in the embers of a kitchen fire, which was referred to as a bean hole. You can still get bean hole suppers to this day.

1 pound dried beans

1 tablespoon unsalted butter

1 cup thinly sliced onion (about 1 small)

6 ounces salt pork, scored

¼ cup molasses

2 tablespoons dark brown sugar, firmly packed

2 tablespoons ketchup or tomato paste

2 teaspoons dry mustard

1 teaspoon kosher or sea salt

1 tablespoon apple cider vinegar

1 Lay out the dry beans on a rimmed baking sheet and remove and discard any debris. Place in a large stockpot and cover with 2 inches of water. Soak 10 to 12 hours and then drain.

2 Heat the oven to 300°F.

3 In a large, oven-proof stockpot over medium heat, melt the butter. Add the onions and gently cook until softened and fragrant, about 10 minutes. Add the salt pork, beans, molasses, brown sugar, ketchup, dry mustard, and salt and stir well to combine. Add enough water to cover by 2 inches (about 1 quart). Cover and bake 4 to 6 hours, checking every hour or so to check the doneness of the beans and adding water as needed. When fully cooked, remove from the oven and let rest about 10 minutes.

4 Stir in the vinegar and serve.

MAIN COURSES

STEAMED LOBSTER

Makes 6 servings

There is no more iconic Maine dish than steamed lobster. This recipe features two primary ingredients: fresh, clean seawater and live Maine lobsters. If seawater is not available, tap water with added sea salt is acceptable. If you have access to rockweed, a type of seaweed (lobsters are often sold with it), add it to the pot. True Mainers recommend steaming lobsters in 2 to 3 inches of water in the bottom of a lobster pot, preferably on top of a nest of rockweed or a wire rack.

Lobsters that are 1¼ to 1½ pounds are a good size for one person, and they should be tender and sweet. If you like culls (one-clawed lobsters) at those weights, you're really in for a treat—extra body and tail meat.

It can get messy, so cover the table with newspapers and wear a bib (and goggles if necessary).

About 2 pounds rockweed, optional

About 5 cups fresh Maine seawater or tap water with 1 tablespoon sea salt

6 1¼- to 1½-pound live Maine lobsters

Drawn Butter (page 47) for serving

1 In a lobster pot or very large stockpot, make a nest out of rockweed if using. Pour about 3 inches of water in the pot, cover, place over high heat, and bring the water to a boil. Carefully place the lobsters over the rockweed. Cover and steam for 10 minutes. Uncover and check the lobsters: they should be completely red in color, their tails should be tightly curled, and their front "legs" should remove easily by twisting them away from the body. If the lobsters are not fully cooked, return to the heat for another 5 minutes.

2 Carefully remove the lobsters to a platter or 6 plates and serve with Drawn Butter (page 47).

SEAFOOD BAKE

Makes 6 servings

A traditional seaside seafood bake is an all-day affair that requires digging a deep hole in the wet sand; gathering and heating special rocks; burying the hot rocks in the sand pit with the seafood; and baking the seafood in the hot rocks. It's always a fun adventure, but it requires a Herculean amount of effort and a boatload of ingredients. This recipe includes all the elements with just a bit of the fuss.

Rockweed is a type of seaweed that is traditionally used for seafood baking and steaming. If you're unable to forage your own, ask your fishmonger—lobsters are often transported in it.

About 3 pounds fresh rockweed or other seaweed, well-rinsed

1 pound small (golf ball–sized) new potatoes

6 chicken thighs

3 1¼- to 1½-pound Maine lobsters

6 ears husked corn

2 pounds medium (3-inch) soft- or hard-shell clams

2 pounds mussels, rinsed and de-bearded

1½ to 2 cups Drawn Butter (page 47), optional

1 Place the rockweed in a large stockpot and cover with water. Soak for 1 hour.

2 Drain and discard the water and set the wet rockweed aside. In the same pot over medium heat, bring 8 cups of salted water to a boil. Add the potatoes and chicken and boil about 10 minutes (the potatoes and chicken will not be fully cooked). Drain and discard the water; set chicken and potatoes aside.

3 Heat a live wood fire or gas grill to medium-high.

4 Place a 4-inch-high layer of the damp rockweed over the grill surface. Place the lobsters in the center of the grill, on top of the rockweed, and surround the lobster with corn. Arrange the potatoes and chicken in layers over the lobsters. Top with the clams and mussels. Completely cover all with the remaining rockweed. Close the lid and cook for about 45 minutes or until the shellfish have opened and the lobsters are red in color, their tails are tightly curled, and their front "legs" remove easily by twisting them away from the body. Discard the rockweed.

5 Split the lobsters in half lengthwise and arrange all seafood bake ingredients on a large platter or individual plates. Serve immediately with Drawn Butter, if desired.

· · ·

DRAWN BUTTER

1 pound (4 sticks) unsalted butter

In a small saucepan over medium heat, melt the butter. Simmer until the cloudy milk solids separate and sink to the bottom of the pan. Remove from the heat and strain the clear, yellow liquid into a glass jar; discard the white, cloudy bits. Once cooled, cover and refrigerate until ready to use.

LOBSTER ROLL

Makes 6 servings

For many Maine-lovers, a heap of sweet lobster meat piled onto a soft, buttery bun is one of life's great pleasures—especially when eaten with a beautiful coastal view. There are a lot of ways to make a lobster roll, and in Maine, it is a point of much debate. Too many flavors and too much mayonnaise can overwhelm the subtle flavor of the lobster.

This lobster roll recipe is straightforward, so you really taste the fresh lobster.

2 pounds cooked lobster
meat, roughly chopped

3 tablespoons chopped parsley

3 tablespoons chopped
celery leaves

About ¾ cup mayonnaise

2 tablespoons
unsalted butter

6 New England–style
hot dog buns

6 pieces
Boston (bibb) lettuce

1 In a medium bowl, combine the lobster meat, parsley, and celery leaves. Add half the mayonnaise and taste; the mixture should have just enough mayonnaise to hold the ingredients together, but lobster should be the predominant flavor. Add more mayonnaise if necessary.

2 Generously butter the hot dog buns on both sides of the outside of the bun.

3 In a medium sauté pan over medium-high heat, brown the rolls on both sides. Lay 1 piece of lettuce in each bun and evenly divide the lobster mixture among the hot dog rolls. Serve.

Note: True Maine lobster rolls are served on New England or Frankfurter rolls, which have flat sides that can be buttered and then grilled or toasted.

MOXIE-BRAISED PULLED PORK SANDWICHES

with Asian Red Cabbage Cole Slaw

Makes 8 servings

Soda, especially Moxie (see page 23), may seem like an unconventional ingredient for pulled pork, but its herbaceous notes and high sugar content adds lovely flavor to the aromatics in this braising liquid. This is all about low-and-slow cooking. To develop deep flavors in this tough cut of meat, it must be gently cooked for 4 to 5 hours.

FOR THE BRAISE

1 can Moxie soda

1 cup homemade or low-sodium chicken stock

1 cup thinly sliced yellow onion (about 1 medium)

2 tablespoons minced garlic (about 2 cloves)

2 tablespoons chili powder

2 teaspoons ground cumin

2 teaspoons kosher or sea salt

4- to 5-pound bone-in pork shoulder (Boston butt)

FOR THE COLE SLAW

2 cups thinly sliced red cabbage

1 cup thinly sliced green cabbage

½ medium red onion, thinly sliced

½ cup freshly grated carrots

½ cup roughly chopped dry-roasted peanuts or toasted cashew nuts

¼ cup low-sodium soy sauce

3 tablespoons rice wine vinegar

2 tablespoons vegetable oil

1 tablespoon minced fresh ginger

1 tablespoon minced garlic

1 tablespoon light brown sugar, densely packed

1 teaspoon toasted sesame oil

6 sesame-seed hamburger buns

Make the braise:

1 Heat the oven to 250°F. Position a rack in the middle of the oven.

2 In a large casserole dish, combine the Moxie, stock, onion, garlic, chili powder, cumin, and salt. Place the pork in the dish and roll around a few times until well coated. Place in the oven and bake 5 to 6 hours, turning and basting the meat every 30 minutes. Bake until the meat easily shreds apart.

3 Remove the meat to a cutting board and let rest 15 minutes. Strain the liquid into a large saucepan and discard the solids. Place saucepan over high heat and bring to a boil; cook until the liquid is reduced by half.

Make the coleslaw:

1 In a medium bowl, combine all the coleslaw ingredients and toss until well combined.

2 Serve: Using a fork, shred the meat and add it to the reduced pan juices. Stir well to coat. Serve on the buns with a few spoonfuls of slaw on top of the pork or on the side.

MAPLE AND SOY-GLAZED WHOLE ROASTED SALMON

with Pan-Seared Wild Mushrooms

Makes 8 servings

Maple syrup is graded differently in every state, but in Maine, it's all grade A. Depending on your preference, grade A maple syrup comes in many varieties: golden with a delicate flavor, amber with a rich flavor, dark with a robust flavor, or very dark with a strong flavor. Golden or amber is suggested for this recipe, as the syrup is reduced, thus concentrating its maple flavor.

Wild Maine salmon is getting harder and harder to find, but farmed salmon is quite abundant. Both can be excellent, depending on how and where they were raised. Maine mushrooms in hundreds of varieties appear in damp forests from early spring through late fall. These include: hen of the wood, oyster, porcini, chanterelles, morels, and more. If you forage, do it with an expert, or simply look for wild mushrooms at the many farmers' markets up and down the coast.

FOR THE FISH

½ cup golden or amber maple syrup

¼ cup low-sodium soy sauce

1 tablespoon chopped fresh ginger

1 tablespoon rice wine vinegar

1 4- to 6-pound whole salmon, cleaned and scaled

About 1 tablespoon vegetable oil

FOR THE MUSHROOMS

1 pound wild mushrooms, cut into 1-inch pieces

1 cup thinly sliced leek, white and light green parts only (about 2 3-inch pieces)

3 tablespoons vegetable oil

1 tablespoon minced fresh ginger

1 tablespoon minced garlic

1 tablespoon low-sodium soy sauce

Make the fish:

1 In a small saucepan over medium-high heat, combine the maple syrup, ¼ cup soy sauce, 1 tablespoon chopped ginger, and rice wine vinegar. Bring to a boil and reduce to a simmer. Cook until reduced by half and thickened, about 5 minutes. Strain the liquid into a bowl, discard the solids, and let cool.

2 Heat the oven to 400°F. Place racks in the middle and lower third of the oven.

3 Gently pat the fish dry and generously oil it on both sides. Transfer to a rimmed baking sheet or large roasting pan and place on the middle rack; roast for 15 minutes.

4 Remove from the oven and baste with reserved maple and soy sauce mixture. Return to the oven and cook 15 minutes more, until flesh is opaque and reaches an internal temperature of 120°F (for

Continued

rare). Remove from the oven and baste with more of the maple and soy sauce mixture. Let rest 10 minutes; reserve any leftover sauce.

Make the mushrooms:

1 While the fish is roasting, combine all the mushroom ingredients in a large bowl. Spread evenly on a rimmed baking sheet and place on the lower oven rack. Roast about 10 minutes, remove from the oven, and shake the pan to redistribute.

2 Return to the oven and roast until the mushrooms soften and are lightly browned in places and garlic and ginger are fragrant, about 10 minutes more. Remove from the oven to a serving platter or bowl.

3 Serve fish on a large platter with mushrooms and sauce on the side.

LOBSTER POT PIE

Makes 4 servings

This recipe is an elegant presentation, yet it's simple to prepare. Everyone should make puff pastry from scratch once in their lives, but store-bought frozen puff pastry is much quicker and easier. These individual pies freeze well (before baking) for a showstopper impromptu meal or special occasion, and this recipe can be easily multiplied.

3 tablespoons unsalted butter

1 cup thinly sliced leek, white and light green parts only (about 2 3-inch pieces)

½ cup minced carrot (about 1 medium)

½ cup minced celery (about 1 rib)

¼ cup brandy or Cognac

1 clove garlic, lightly crushed

2 tablespoons all-purpose flour, plus more for dusting

1¾ cups heavy cream

Few grates fresh nutmeg

Kosher or sea salt

White pepper

1 pound uncooked lobster meat, cut into ¾-inch pieces

1 14-ounce package frozen puff pastry, thawed

1 large egg white, beaten

1 In a medium saucepan over medium heat, melt the butter. Add the leek, carrot, and celery and cook until the vegetables are softened and fragrant, about 15 minutes. Add the brandy and garlic and cook until the liquid is reduced by half, about 10 minutes.

2 Whisk in the 2 tablespoons flour and cook, stirring frequently, about 2 minutes, taking care not to brown. Slowly whisk in the

Continued

cream. Grate in the nutmeg and bring to a simmer. Cook, stirring occasionally, until sauce is thickened, about 4 minutes.

3 Remove and discard the garlic and season with salt and white pepper. Stir in the lobster and remove from the heat.

4 Heat the oven to 425°F.

5 Evenly divide the lobster mixture among four 8-ounce ramekins or oven-proof bowls and place on a rimmed baking sheet.

6 On a lightly floured surface, roll out the pastry dough to a ⅛-inch thickness. Cut out four circles in the shape of the baking dishes that are 1 inch wider than the tops of the dishes. Brush the edges of the dishes with the egg white and lay the pastry rounds over the lobster mixtures, leaving 1-inch overhangs. Brush pastry rounds with egg white and make a few vent holes in the pastry. Decorate the tops with any leftover dough. Bake until the pastry is golden brown on top, 20 to 25 minutes. Remove from the oven and serve hot.

TOURTIERE

Makes about 10 servings

Tourtiere, a traditional Quebecoise Christmas dish, is usually served at the feast following midnight church services. As Maine borders Canada, this hearty and delicious tradition has made its way into Maine culture and can be found throughout the year in many bakeries.

Seasoned pork and starches (by way of chopped or mashed potatoes or rolled oats) are the centerpiece of this stick-to-your-ribs crowd pleaser. Tourtiere can be made in individual portions and it freezes quite well before or after being baked.

FOR THE PASTRY

3 cups all-purpose flour

2 teaspoons kosher or sea salt

10 ounces (2½ sticks) cold unsalted butter, cubed

2 large egg yolks

5 tablespoons very cold whole milk

FOR THE FILLING

1 tablespoon olive oil

2 pounds ground pork (or a combination of ground pork and ground beef)

1 cup finely chopped onion (about 1 large)

½ cup finely chopped celery (about 1 rib)

2 tablespoons minced garlic

2 cups peeled and diced (¼-inch) potatoes (about 1 pound), reserved in water to cover

½ teaspoon ground cloves

½ teaspoon ground cinnamon

Few grates fresh nutmeg

Kosher or sea salt

Freshly ground black pepper

1 large egg white, lightly beaten

Continued

Make the pastry:

1 In the bowl of a food processor, pulse together the flour and 2 teaspoons salt a few times. Add the butter and pulse a few times more, just until the butter is broken up into pea-sized pieces.

2 In a medium bowl, beat together the egg yolks and milk. Add the mixture to the food processor and pulse a few times, until the dough just barely holds together.

3 Turn out the dough onto a clean, lightly floured work surface and roughly push it around, without kneading, just until it holds together. Form dough into two equal-sized balls and wrap in plastic wrap; refrigerate 1 hour or up to overnight.

4 Remove the dough from the refrigerator 10 to 15 minutes before using.

Make the filling:

1 In a large sauté pan over medium-high heat, warm the oil. Add the meat and cook until brown on one side, about 3 minutes. Turn over and break up into small pieces using a spatula or spoon and cook until still slightly pink, about 10 minutes. Using a slotted spoon, remove the meat to a bowl and discard all but 1 tablespoon fat. Set aside.

2 Add the onion, celery, and garlic to the pan and cook until the garlic is fragrant, about 2 minutes. Stir in the potatoes, cloves, cinnamon, and nutmeg, along with about 1 tablespoon potato soaking water. Season with salt and pepper and cook until most of the moisture has evaporated, about 5 minutes. Remove from the heat and stir in the meat.

3 Heat the oven to 375°F.

4 On a lightly floured surface, roll out the dough in two 11-inch-wide, ¼-inch-thick rounds.

5 Line a 9-inch pie pan with one dough round, letting the excess dough hang over the rim of the pan. Spoon the filling into the pan. Lay the second piece of dough over the top and tuck the overhang of the bottom piece of dough over the edge of the top crust, pinching and crimping to seal. Brush the top of the pastry with egg white and make a few vent holes in the pastry. Decorate the tops with any leftover dough. Bake until the pastry is golden brown on top, about 45 minutes. Remove from the oven and allow to cool for 10 to 15 minutes before serving.

BAKED SCALLOPS
with Maine Potatoes Au Gratin

Makes 6 servings

Maine scallops are a winter dish harvested for a few short months, usually beginning in November. The scallops are caught within three miles of the Maine coastline, so they are always a "day boat" catch and do not need to be frozen or treated with chemical preservatives to keep them plump and juicy. Scallops have a sweet, nutlike taste that pairs best with subtle flavors.

¼ cup mascarpone cheese

¼ cup dry white wine

2 tablespoons whole milk or cream

2 teaspoons freshly grated lemon zest

Kosher or sea salt

White pepper

2 pounds bay scallops, "foot" or side muscles removed

½ cup unseasoned breadcrumbs

½ cup grated Parmesan

¼ cup melted unsalted butter, plus more for greasing the dish

2 teaspoons red pepper flakes

Garnish: 2 tablespoons chopped fresh flat-leaf parsley

1 recipe Maine Potatoes Au Gratin (page 30) for serving

1 Heat the oven to 400°F.

2 In a medium bowl, whisk together the mascarpone cheese, wine, milk, and lemon zest; season with salt and pepper. Add the scallops and thoroughly but gently coat them with the mixture.

3 In a small bowl, combine the breadcrumbs, Parmesan, ¼ cup butter, and red pepper flakes. Grease the bottom and sides of a shallow baking dish with the extra butter.

4 Arrange the scallops in the baking dish in an even layer. Pour the remaining mascarpone mixture over the top. Top with the breadcrumb mixture and bake until the breadcrumbs are lightly browned, about 10 minutes.

5 Adjust the oven to broil and broil until the breadcrumbs are well browned, about 1 minute more. Sprinkle with parsley and serve immediately with Maine Potatoes Au Gratin.

SHRIMP AND PEA WIGGLE

Makes 6 servings

Shrimp and Pea Wiggle is an old-school New England recipe that found a foothold in Maine. It was typically served on top of rice, mashed potatoes, or crackers and is said to have been a favorite of Eleanor Roosevelt.

About the wiggle? When the shrimp get added to the pan, they curl up and wiggle a bit from the heat. Just saying "wiggle," you can't help but giggle.

5 tablespoons unsalted butter	1 cup heavy cream
2 tablespoons finely chopped shallots	1 teaspoon tomato paste
1 pound fresh medium shrimp, peeled and deveined	2 cups fresh or frozen peas
	Kosher or sea salt
3 tablespoons all-purpose flour	Freshly ground black pepper
1 cup fish stock	Cooked potatoes or rice or crackers for serving

1 In a large sauté pan over medium heat, melt 2 tablespoons butter. Add the shallots and cook until softened and fragrant, about 2 minutes. Raise the heat to high, add the shrimp, and cook just until pink, opaque, and tightly curled, about 5 minutes, being careful not to overcook. Remove from the heat and set aside.

2 In a separate saucepan over medium heat, melt the remaining 3 tablespoons butter. Slowly whisk in the flour and cook until thickened, 2 to 3 minutes. Slowly whisk in the fish stock and then the cream.

3 Remove about ½ cup thickened mixture to a small bowl and stir in the tomato paste. Whisk the bowl contents back into the saucepan. Stir in the peas and cook over low heat until it reaches the desired consistency, another 4 or 5 minutes. Season to taste with salt and black pepper. Fold in the shrimp and shallots.

4 Serve over cooked potatoes or rice or crackers.

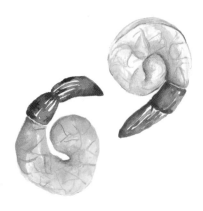

DESSERTS

WHOOPIE PIES

Makes 8 servings

Like many good things from the kitchen, whoopie pies were invented via a clever use of leftovers—in this case, leftover chocolate cake batter spooned into rounds and later filled with fluffy leftover cake frosting. Just imagine: a chocolate sandwich. The kids in Maine who got these treats in their lunchboxes or as an after-school snack would exclaim, "Whoopie!" Vegetable shortening and marshmallow fluff have been the traditional filling ingredients, but butter tastes better than shortening (the marshmallow fluff is just too delicious to change.) Labadie's Bakery in Lewiston, Maine, has been selling whoopie pies since 1925.

FOR THE CAKE

1 cup densely packed light brown sugar

8 tablespoons (1 stick) unsalted butter, room temperature

1 cup buttermilk

1 whole large egg

1 teaspoon vanilla extract

2 cups all-purpose flour

½ cup Dutch-process cocoa powder

1¼ teaspoons baking soda

1 teaspoon kosher or sea salt

FOR THE FILLING

2 cups marshmallow creme, such as Fluff brand

1 cup confectioners' sugar

8 tablespoons (1 stick) unsalted butter, softened

1 teaspoon vanilla extract

Make the cake:

1 Heat the oven to 350°F.

2 In the bowl of a stand mixer fitted with the whisk attachment, beat together the brown sugar and 1 stick butter until pale and fluffy. Beat in the buttermilk, egg, and vanilla.

3 In a small bowl, whisk together the flour, cocoa, baking soda, and salt. In batches, gradually add the dry ingredients to the stand mixer bowl as it runs, occasionally scraping down the sides of the bowl. Mix just until the dry ingredients are fully incorporated.

4 Line a rimmed baking sheet with lightly greased parchment or wax paper. Using a large ice cream scoop or ¼-cup measure, pour domes of the batter onto the baking sheet, leaving 2 inches of space in between. Bake until the tops are puffed and cakes spring back when touched, about 12 minutes. Remove from the oven, let cool 5 minutes, and then transfer to a cooling rack to cool completely.

Make the filling:

1 In the clean bowl of a stand mixer fitted with the whisk attachment, beat together all the filling ingredients until smooth.

2 Spread the filling on the flat sides of half the cooled cakes and top with the remaining cakes. Serve.

BLUEBERRY ALMOND STREUSEL CAKE

Makes 12 servings

Maine blueberries are a good idea for most traditional baked goods, be it a pie, slump, grunt, cobbler, crisp, or cake. Here, they marry well in an easy cake with a bit of almond and crunchy topping for an anytime snack or dessert, but possibly the best friend for a cup of coffee or tea.

FOR THE STREUSEL TOPPING

½ cup granulated sugar

6 tablespoons all-purpose flour

2 tablespoons finely ground almond meal

Pinch of kosher or sea salt

2 tablespoons unsalted butter, cut into small pieces

FOR THE CAKE

8 tablespoons (1 stick) unsalted butter, at room temperature, plus more for the pan

1 cup all-purpose flour, plus more for the pan

½ cup finely ground almond meal

2 teaspoons baking powder

½ teaspoon kosher or sea salt

1 cup granulated sugar

2 whole large eggs

½ teaspoon almond extract

½ cup sour cream or plain yogurt

2 cups blueberries

Make the streusel:

In a small bowl, using a fork, mash the sugar, flour, almond meal, salt, and butter together until well mixed but still crumbly.

Make the cake:

1 Heat the oven to 350°F. Line the bottom of an 8-inch square pan with parchment paper. Butter and flour the parchment, as well as the bottom and sides of the pan.

2 In another small bowl, whisk together 1 cup flour, almond meal, baking powder, and salt. In the bowl of a standing mixer with the whisk attachment (or using a handheld blender), beat together the butter and sugar until pale and fluffy. Beat in the eggs one at a time, scraping down the bowl between each addition. Add the almond extract. Add one-third of the flour mixture, all of the sour cream, and another third of the flour, mixing just until blended. Stir in the remaining flour. Gently fold in the blueberries.

3 Spread the cake batter into the prepared cake pan. Scatter the streusel topping over the top. Bake until the top is golden brown and an inserted toothpick comes out clean, about 35 minutes. Cool the cake in the pan on a rack for about 10 minutes, then slice and serve.

BLUEBERRY JAM

Makes ten ½-pint jars

Summer in a jar.

10 cups fresh wild blueberries

6 cups granulated sugar

2 tablespoons freshly grated lemon zest

½ teaspoon kosher or sea salt

⅓ cup freshly squeezed lemon juice

1 Place about three-quarters of the berries in a large stockpot and lightly mash them (do not puree). Stir in the remaining berries, sugar, lemon zest, and salt. Place the pot over medium-high heat and cook, stirring occasionally, until the mixture comes to a gentle simmer. Reduce the heat to a simmer, stirring often, until the berries have thickened, 25 to 30 minutes (depending on how much moisture is in the berries). Stir in the lemon juice and cook an additional 5 minutes. Remove from the heat.

2 Ladle the jam into ten ½-pint sterilized glass jars, leaving ¼ inch of head space in each jar. Gently tap each jar on the counter to force out air bubbles and wipe rims with a clean towel. Apply a lid and ring to each jar and process jars in boiling water for 10 minutes. Remove the jars and let cool.

3 Properly sealed, jars can be stored 6 to 8 months; unsealed or unprocessed jars must be refrigerated.

MAPLE TARTE TATIN

Makes one 12-inch pie

A classic tart Tatin is an upside-down apple pie originating from the kitchen of the Tatin sisters of France, who were turn-of-the-century hotel proprietors. Apples get poached in a heady caramel sauce and then placed in a pie plate and covered with pastry. Once it's fully cooked, the pie is flipped. This recipe cuts out the poaching and gets a Downeast twist with the addition of maple syrup.

Hundreds of apple varieties grow in Maine. Some trees bear ripe fruit as early as late August, while others peak toward the end of October. You can find everything from sweet to tart to juicy to crisp, and some are better than others for baking. For this recipe, firm apples, such as an Empire Gravenstein or Northern Spy, work best. Serve with vanilla, ginger, or cinnamon ice cream.

1 14-ounce package frozen puff pastry, thawed

All-purpose flour, for dusting

4 tablespoons (½ stick) unsalted butter, cut into ¼-inch cubes

2 tablespoons granulated sugar

½ teaspoon ground cinnamon (or dried ginger or a combination of both)

About 2 pounds firm apples, peeled, cored, and sliced into ½-inch wedges

2 tablespoons golden or amber maple syrup

1 Heat the oven to 425°F.

2 On a lightly floured surface, roll out the pastry dough to a ⅛-inch thickness. Using a 12-inch pie plate as a guide, cut out a round that is 1 inch wider (13 inches total) than the pie plate. Keep chilled until ready to use.

3 Dot the bottom of the pie plate with 4 or 5 cubes butter.

4 In a small bowl, combine the sugar and cinnamon. Arrange the apple slices on the bottom of the pie plate by shingling them together in a single layer. Dot the first apple layer with 4 or 5 pieces butter and about 1 tablespoon syrup. Sprinkle a light layer of cinnamon sugar on top. Repeat until all the ingredients are used.

5 Cover the apples with the reserved pastry round, tucking the outer edge of the pastry under the apples. Bake until the pastry is light golden, about 10 minutes.

6 Reduce the oven temperature to 375°F and bake until the pastry is puffed and light brown, about 20 minutes longer. Remove from the oven and let cool for 10 minutes.

7 Lay a serving plate larger than the pie plate on top of the tarte Tatin and carefully flip over so the tarte Tatin is apple side up on the serving plate. Remove the pie plate. Serve.

PLOYES

(Buckwheat Crepes with Blueberry Jam)

Makes about 2 dozen

The ploye is a terrific culinary gem that hails from the mixed traditions of northern Maine along the Canadian border—particularly the town of Madawaska, where buckwheat flour is grown and milled. Ployes are similar to crepes or thin pancakes, but they are not flipped, so they have the appearance of a thin crumpet.

When making ployes, look for the many bubbles that form on top, which are referred to as the "eyes." It is customary to serve ployes with butter and a bit of maple sugar or syrup, but try them with blueberry jam.

1¼ cups light buckwheat flour	About ¾ cup hot water
1 cup unbleached, all-purpose flour	Unsalted butter for serving
1 tablespoon baking powder	About 1 cup Blueberry Jam (page 70) for serving
1 teaspoon kosher or sea salt	
¾ cup cold water	

1 In a large bowl, combine the flours, baking powder, and salt. Slowly whisk in the cold water, making a wet paste. Whisk in the hot water, ¼ cup at a time, until the consistency is like wet paint—it's okay if there are a few lumps. Let the batter rest 1 hour.

Continued

2 Warm a cast-iron skillet over medium-high heat (ployes are not flipped, so be careful not to raise the heat too high or they will burn before the tops cook through). Ladle a 6-inch circle of batter into the center of the pan and as it cooks, watch for the many air bubbles or "eyes." When the ploye top has cooked and is no longer wet, remove to a plate and keep warm. Repeat until all the batter is used. Remove from the heat.

3 Butter each ploye and spoon 1 tablespoon or more of the Blueberry Jam into the center of each. Roll or fold into quarters and serve.

NATIVE PUDDING

Makes 8 servings

When the British colonists came to New England, they had trouble getting wheat crops started, so they relied on the local tradition of growing corn. Those with a sweet tooth mashed cornmeal and maple syrup together into what became known as Indian Pudding which is often sweet, heavy and grainy. This modern version features traditional flavors but is lighter and more elegant.

3 cups whole milk

2 tablespoons unsalted butter, plus more for preparing the ramekins

1½ cups finely ground cornmeal

2½ tablespoons powdered gelatin bloomed in 1 cup cold water

⅓ cup golden maple syrup

1 whole large egg, beaten

2 tablespoons molasses

1 teaspoon ground ginger

¼ teaspoon kosher or sea salt

1 cup whipped cream for serving

2 tablespoons minced candied ginger for serving

1 In a heavy-bottomed saucepan over high heat, bring the milk and 2 tablespoons butter to a simmer. Whisk in the cornmeal and reduce heat to low. Simmer until the mixture begins to thicken, about 5 minutes. Remove from the heat and whisk in the bloomed gelatin, maple syrup, egg, molasses, ginger, and salt.

2 Grease eight ½-cup ramekins with remaining butter. Pour the conrmeal mixture into prepared ramekins and refrigerate until set, about 30 minutes.

3 Top with whipped cream and sprinkle with ginger.

POPOVERS

with Strawberry Ginger Jam

Makes about 12 servings

Since the late 1800s, it's been a summer tradition to enjoy tea with popovers and strawberry jam on the lawn of the Jordan Pond House at Acadia National Park. For many, it's a welcome reward after hiking the Bubbles mountain range; for others, it's a chance to relax and take in the magnificent scenery of Acadia.

3 tablespoons unsalted butter, melted and cooled to room temperature, plus more for greasing

3 whole large eggs

1 cup whole milk

1 cup all-purpose flour

½ teaspoon kosher or sea salt

8 tablespoons (1 stick) unsalted butter, for serving

Strawberry Ginger Jam (recipe follows)

1 Heat the oven to 375°F. Grease a muffin pan with some of the melted butter.

2 In the bowl of a stand mixer fitted with the whisk attachment or with a handheld mixer, beat the eggs on low speed until frothy. Add the milk and remaining 3 tablespoons melted butter and beat until well combined.

3 In a small bowl, combine the flour and salt. Gradually beat the flour mixture into the egg mixture, just until smooth.

4 Pour batter halfway up each of the prepared muffin pan cups. Bake until golden brown and puffed, 45 minutes. Remove from the oven.

5 Carefully make a small slit on the top of each popover to release steam. Return to the oven and bake until deep brown, 10 minutes more. Immediately remove the popovers from the muffin pan, using a spatula if necessary.

6 Serve hot with butter and Strawberry Ginger Jam.

• • •

STRAWBERRY GINGER JAM

Makes six ½-pint jars

3 pounds strawberries, hulled and coarsely chopped

2½ cups granulated sugar

½ cup freshly squeezed lemon juice

3 tablespoons finely chopped fresh ginger

1 In a heavy-bottomed saucepan over medium heat, combine the strawberries, sugar, lemon juice, and ginger. Cook, stirring occasionally, just until the sugar melts.

2 Raise the heat to medium-high and bring the mixture to a boil. Continue to boil, stirring frequently and mashing the strawberries as you stir, until the jam is thickened and bubbles completely cover the surface, about 10 minutes.

3 Ladle the preserves into six ½-pint sterilized glass jars, leaving ¼ inch of head space at the top of each jar. Gently tap each jar on a counter to force out air bubbles and wipe the rims with a clean towel. Apply the lid and ring to each jar and process the jars in boiling water for 10 minutes. Remove the jars and let cool.

4 Properly sealed, jars can be stored 6 to 8 months; unsealed or unprocessed jars must be refrigerated.

ACKNOWLEDGMENTS

I am grateful to my extraordinary family, especially my kind, generous, creative, adventurous, and intelligent parents who spent their honeymoon on Mount Desert Island and who cast a large safety net for me; my siblings and cousins, who do their best to keep my ego in check; my nieces, nephews, and godchildren, who fill my heart when I cook for them; and my extraordinary friends, who indulge my whims and keep me safe.

Special thanks for the extra insight into Maine cooking traditions from my dear friends Carolyn Morrell, Helen Gallo Bryan, Nancy Harmon Jenkins, Mary Dumont, Jeremy Sewall, Patty "Noma" Arcuni, Randy Hammond, Jennifer Skiff, Axie Diana, and Cindy Joyce.

Also the greatest champion of this small but mighty book has to be the ever-cheerful, level-headed, and supportive Leslie Jonath.

Courtney Jentzen would like to thank Carly Martin for her help with the illustrations. Thanks also to Redding, Stevie, and Paul.

INDEX